Melania Trump:

Everything you ever wanted to know about America's future first lady

Talia Rose

Dedicated to all the courageous women out there

Table of Contents

1. Introduction

Melania Trump's journey started in Slovenia a communist country. Even though, she had a simple childhood, her parents were extremely supportive of her. Her determination and exceptional looks soon pulled her into the modelling career which eventually landed her in New York City via Rome and Paris. In an almost fairy tale like story, she met one of the most famous and influential man in New York, Mr. Donald Trump. Her life drastically changed after that and she never had to look back at her humble beginnings. Now, thanks to her husband's popularity and her own personality, there's a greater chance than ever that she might make the move from New York to the White House.

2. A short biography

Melania Trump was born Melanija Knavs on April 26, 1970 in Novo Mesto, Slovenia. Her mother Amalija worked at a children's clothing manufacturer as a patternmaker. She was the first one to introduce Melania to fashion and design. Melania's father Viktor had a different background. He worked as a manager at a car and motorcycle dealership and he was also a member of the communist party. He was a strong role model and taught his daughters Melania and Ines the importance of ethics and hard work.

She grew up in the town of Sevnica scouted off the street by the photographer Stane Jerko and she started modelling in 1987. She never had to look back again. Even though, she did get enrolled at the University of Ljubljana in the architecture and design program, she left after her freshman year to further pursue modelling. She lived and modelled in the fabulous cities of Rome and Paris where she picked up Italian and French respectively. During her modelling career, Melania decided to Germanize her last from Knavs to Knauss by changing the v to a u and by adding an extra s at the end.

Paolo Zampolli, a wealthy Italian businessman named Paolo Zampolli brought Melania to New York over on a modeling contract and a work visa in 1996. Her life took a dramatic turn, when she got introduced to Donald Trump in 1998 at a Fashion week party. It wasn't actually a case of love at first sight and Melania did make Donald work a bit harder than usual, but in no one time she was soon appearing besides her boyfriend in various interviews and events. The couple got married on January 22, 2005 at the Episcopal Church in Palm Beach, Florida. Naturally, it was an extremely lavish ceremony and amongst the many celebrity guests were Senator Hillary Clinton and her husband ex-President Bill Clinton. Melania and Donald's son Barron William Trump was born in 2006.

As a model, Melania has appeared on the covers of various magazines such as Vogue, Harper's Bazaar, British GQ, Ocean Drive, Avenue, In Style, New York Magazine, the Sports Illustrated Swimsuit Issue, Allure, Self, Glamour, Vanity Fair, and Elle. Besides modelling, the five feet eleven inches brunette has also been involved in different organizations and charities some of which are the Martha Graham Dance Company, the Boy's Club of New York, Police Athletic League, Love Our Children USA and the American Red cross.

Melania has a strong business sense like her husband and father. She has a line of jewelry collection with QVC called "Melania™ Timepieces & Jewelry". In addition, she also has her own skin care product named "Melania™ Caviar Complexe C6".

Even though she was always popular in the New York scene, she came to national limelight once Donald Trump started his presidential campaign. She was a subject of an attack ad-campaign and she was constantly being criticized for past modelling career and her accent. However, she did prove to have a very thick skin and easily brush-off the criticism. Like always, she has been a staunch supporter of her husband throughout the campaign. Her supporters love her and take her as an excellent role model for all the women out there. On the other hand, the critics are constantly trying to tarnish her image by focus on her lacking and mistakes. However, it is a fact that, all the faux-pas and controversies asides, both of these groups will admit that she is closer than ever to becoming the first lady of America.

3. The First Speech

Melania gave her first campaign speech at a Milwaukee, Wisconsin Rally on April 4, 2016. Even though the two minute speech mainly focused on her husband, it brought out her own energy, which the crowd loved. Here's the exact transcript of the speech.

Hello. Thank you, we love you too. It is wonderful to be here today with you and with my husband. I'm very proud of him. He's a hard worker. He's kind. He has a great heart. He's tough. He's smart. He's a great communicator. He's a great negotiator. He's telling the truth. He's a great leader. He's fair. As you may know by now, when you attack him, he will punch back ten times harder. No matter who you are, a man or a woman, he treats everyone equally. He's a fighter and if you elect him to be your President, he will fight for you and for our country. He will work for you and with you and together we will make America strong and great again.

4. An interview

One of Melania's most popular interviews was the one she had with MSNBC host Mika Brzezinski that aired on "Morning Joe" on February 24, 2016.

Here's the transcript of the interview. MB = Mika Brzezinski, MT = Melania Trump.

MB: Melania Trump first arrived in the United States from Slovenia back in 1996. And now two decades later, she is facing the prospect of becoming first lady. Yesterday, I sat down with Melania Trump and got her to weigh-in on everything from her husband's rhetoric's surrounding immigration to his propensity for profanity on the stump to his treatment of women. I began by asking her how the entire experience has been so far.

MT: Well, it's amazing what's going on and we're having fun. We like to keep life as normal as possible for my son Barron. And I'm a full time mom and I love it. So I decided not to be in the campaign so much, but I support my husband hundred percent.

MB: We wanna understand who Melania is?

MT: I grew up in Slovenia and I went to school there. I studied design and architecture. And then I moved to Milan and Paris to live there where I had a successful modelling career. I came to New York in 1996.

MB: How many languages do you speak?

MT: I speak a few languages.

MB: A few?

MT: English, Italian, French, German.

MB: Tell me about your mother.

MT: Really special. She is...with a lot of elegance and style. She was in fashion industry for a long time.

MB: What did you father do?

MT: He was a sales person and he was a manager of the company. And once Slovenia separated and it was possible to have own business, he opened his own business.

MB: What was it that you saw in Donald when you met him or fell in love with him?

MT: His mind, amazing mind. And very smart, very charming, a great energy. We have a great relationship. We are own people. I am my own person, he is his own person. And I think that's very important. I don't want to change him, he doesn't want to change me.

MB: I've got a list of terms that have been used to describe your husband from the left, the right and the center. And they're not pretty. From stupid to demagogue, jerk, idiot, racist, sexist, race baiting, xenophobic, vulgarian in chief, textbook narcissist. It goes on. What do you make of all this when you hear it?

MT: It's normal that will come up. We are prepared for that. We have a thick skin and we know that people will judge him and people will call names. And they don't give him enough credit. From June that he announced, they don't give him enough credit.

MB: What about people who feel let's just go down the list because the campaign started and many felt that he had insulted Mexicans.

MT: No, I don't feel he insulted the Mexicans. He said 'illegal immigrants'. He didn't talk about everybody. He talked about illegal immigrants. And after few weeks, after a few weeks of giving him hard time and bashing him in the media, they turned around. They said, "You know what? He's right. He's right what's he talking about. And he opened conversation that nobody did."

MB: But, you're an immigrant.

MT: Yes.

MB: Do you ever think he has gone too far.

MT: I follow the law. I follow a law the way it's supposed to be. I never thought to stay here without papers. I had visa, I travelled every few months back to the country, to Slovenia to stamp the visa. I came back, I applied for the green card. I applied for the citizenship later on after many years of green card. So I went by system, I went by the law. And you should do that. You should not just say, okay let me just stay here. And whatever happens happens.

MB: When he talked about a ban on Muslims, which can't happen for so many reasons. Do you ever think he is going too far with some of these? Do you ever worry about it?

MT: Well what he said is that it will be temporary and it's not for all the Muslims, it's the one. We need to screen them who's coming to the country. He wants to protect America. He wants to protect people of America so we have a country. And keep the country safe. That's very important to him. And what's going on in the world, it's very dangerous. You have people coming in the country, you don't know who they are, you don't know what they will do. And that's why he was talking about it. It's temporary. We need to figure it out how and what we will do that we know who is in this country.

MB: What about some of the language he uses? He curses.

MT: Well, do I agree all the time? With him? No, I don't.

MB: Good.

MT: And I tell him that. I tell him my opinions. I tell him what I think. Sometimes he listens, sometimes he don't.

MB: In what areas do you advise him?

MT: I follow the news from A to Z and I know what's going on. I'm on the phone with my husband, few times a day. He calls me, I call him. I tell him what's going on. He's on the road and I give him my opinions.

MB: Let me ask you about women. He has taken a lot of criticism for fallouts of course during the debate with Megan Kelly. In the Trump organization, how are women treated compared to men?

MT: They are treated equal. I see him in live. He treats women, the same way as men. He will tell you what is in his heart. What he thinks. He will not hold it back if you're a woman. You're human, you're human. It's a woman or a man, there's no difference. You are human.

5. Some Famous Quotes

Nothing demonstrates a person's personality better his or her quotes and comments on the media. Here are twenty famous quotes from Melania:

"I didn't make any changes … I'm against Botox, I'm against injections; I think it's damaging your face, damaging your nerves. It's all me. I will age gracefully, as my mom does." — On rumors that she'd had Botox or a breast augmentation (*GQ*)

"It was kind of a fun experience. We stayed in a hotel. It was clean. It was, I think, a Holiday Inn … It's funny when we go and travel. They don't have five-star hotels there, but you go with it." — On a campaign trip to Iowa (*DuJour*)

"I drink coffee, but I don't drink Starbucks. My son likes it, the what do you call it? The Frappuccino?" — On her coffee preferences (*DuJour*)

"I'm very political. I'm not political in public, I'm political at home."— On whether she talks politics with her husband (*Us Weekly*)

"Let's see — the tweeting." — On the one habit she wishes Donald would give up (*Today* show)

"I don't have a nanny. I have a chef, and I have my assistant, and that's it. I do it myself." — On parenting 10-year-old son Barron (*Harper's Bazaar*)

"This is one of the most expensive cities in the world, so that would [be] very difficult." — On whether she would live in New York City on a $35,000 salary (*New York Magazine*)

"He's not a sweatpants child." — On Barron preferring to wear suits (*GQ*)

"Diet Coke from the classic glass bottles." — On her drink of choice (*New York Magazine*)

"No, he would not change diapers and I was completely fine with that. That was very enjoyable to do for me."— On Donald's lack of diaper duty (*Us Weekly*)

"Isn't he the best? He will be the best president ever. We love you." — Praising Donald after he won the South Carolina Republican primary

"We know people will judge him and call him names. They don't give him enough credit." —On backlash to many of Donald's controversial statements (*MSNBC*)

"I follow the law the way it's supposed to be. ... I applied for a visa. I went by the system. I went by the law, and you should do that." — On her husband's harsh policies on undocumented immigrants while she is an immigrant (*MSNBC*)

"Women are treated equal. He treats women equal." — Defending her husband's treatment of women (*MSNBC*)

"Sometimes it's fun to splurge on a great haircut or treatment. For just your regular cut ... above $200." — On how much is too much to spend on a haircut (*New York Magazine*)

"I don't think they sent a gift. Some people didn't send gifts." — On Hillary and Bill Clinton attending her 2005 wedding (*DuJour*)

"Do I agree with everything he says? No. I have my own opinions too, and I tell him that. Sometimes he takes it in and listens, and sometimes he doesn't." — On whether she disagrees with the presidential hopeful (*Us Weekly*)

"I don't see myself as their mother. I am their friend, and I'm here when they need me." — On her relationship with her stepchildren Donald Jr., Ivanka, Eric and Tiffany (*Harper's Bazaar*)

"And he's not lucky?" — Her response to an *Apprentice* contestant telling her she's lucky to live in a mansion during a televised tour of Trump Towers

"We know what our roles are and we are happy with them. I think the mistake some people make is they try to change the man they love after they get married. You cannot change a person." — On the secret to a happy marriage (*Parenting*)

6. What makes her unique

Just like her husband, Melania never fails to stand out from the crowd. Here are a few points that put her in a completely different league when compare to all the other American first ladies.

She could be the only first lady who has posed nude: Melania was photographed by GQ magazine in 2000. A famous image was that of her handcuffed to a briefcase on board of Donald Trump's private jet. Of course, her famous nude photo on the bearskin rug was also from the same photo shoot.

She could be most stylist first lady ever: Jackie Kennedy, JFK's iconic wife was well known for her style and is the most fashionable first lady up to now. Melania, being an ex-super model will definitely put that to the test. Let's not forget that she did have her own line of jewellery and watches.

She speaks five languages: The languages she speak are Slovenian, English, French, Serbian and German. She also mentioned that she spoke Italian in a recent interview. Her command of multiple languages will definitely make her popular with the guests in the White House. Even though she has a thick accent, she is very calm and poised speaker.

She grew up in a communist country: She might be living in New York, but she actually grew up in Slovenia which used to be a part of the communist country Yugoslavia back in the days. She has the chance to become only the second first lady to be born abroad. The only other first lady to be born outside the States was sixth President John Qunicy's wife Louisa Adams, who was English.

7. The Last speech

Melania Trump recently came into the spotlight after giving a short speech at Republican National Convention on July 18, 2016. Here's the exact transcript of the speech.

Thank you very much. Thank you. You have all been very kind to Donald and me, to our young son Barron, and to our whole family. It was very nice welcome and we're excited to be with you at this historic convention. I am so proud of your choice for President of the United States, my husband, Donald J. Trump. And I can assure you, he is moved by this great honor. The 2016 Republican primaries were fierce and started with many candidates, 17 to be exact, and I know that Donald agrees with me when I mention how talented all of them are. They deserve respect and gratitude from all of us. However, when it comes to my husband, I will say that I am definitely biased, and for good reason. I have been with Donald for 18 years and I have been aware of his love for this country since we first met. He never had a hidden agenda when it comes to his patriotism, because, like me, he loves this country so much. I was born in Slovenia, a small, beautiful and then communist country in Central Europe. My sister Ines, who is an incredible woman and a friend, and I were raised by my wonderful parents. My elegant and hard-working mother Amalia introduced me to fashion and beauty. My father Viktor instilled in me a passion for business and travel. Their integrity, compassion and intelligence reflect to this day on me and for my love of family and America. From a young age, my parents impressed on me the values that you work hard for what you want in life: that your word is your bond and you do what you say and keep your promise; that you treat people with respect. They taught and showed me values and morals in their daily life. That is a lesson that I continue to pass along to our son, and we need to pass those lessons on to the many generation to follow.

I travelled the world while working hard in the incredible arena of fashion. After living and working in Milan and Paris, I arrived in New York City twenty years ago, and I saw both the joys and the hardships of daily life. On July 28th, 2006, I was very proud to become a citizen of the United States -- the greatest privilege on planet Earth. I cannot, or will not, take the freedoms this country offers for granted. But these freedoms have come with a price so many times. The sacrifices made by our veterans are reminders to us of this. I would like to take this moment to recognize an amazing veteran, the great Senator Bob Dole. And let us thank all of our veterans in the arena today, and those across our great country. We are all truly blessed to be here. That will never change.

I can tell you with certainty that my husband has been concerned about our country for as long as I have known him. With all of my heart, I know that he will make a great and lasting difference. Donald has a deep and unbounding determination and a never-give-up attitude. I have seen him fight for years to get a project done — or even started — and he does not give up! If you want someone to fight for you and your country, I can assure you, he is the 'guy'. He will never, ever, give up. And, most importantly, he will never, ever, let you down. Donald is, and always has been, an amazing leader. Now, he will go to work for you. His achievements speak for themselves, and his performance throughout the primary campaign proved that he knows how to win. He also knows how to remain focused on improving our country — on keeping it safe and secure. He is tough when he has to be but he is also kind and fair and caring. This kindness is not always noted, but it is there for all to see. That is one reason I fell in love with him to begin with. Donald is intensely loyal. To family, friends, employees, country. He has the utmost respect for his parents, Mary and Fred, to his sisters Maryanne and Elizabeth, to his brother Robert and to the memory of his late brother Fred. His children have been cared for and mentored to the extent that even his adversaries admit they are an amazing testament to who he is as a man and a father. There is a great deal of love in the Trump family. That is our bond, and that is our strength.

Yes, Donald thinks big, which is especially important when considering the presidency of the United States. No room for small thinking. No room for small results. Donald gets things done. Our country is underperforming and needs new leadership. Leadership is also what the world needs. Donald wants our country to move forward in the most positive of ways. Everyone wants change. Donald is the only one that can deliver it. We should not be satisfied with stagnation. Donald wants prosperity for *all* Americans. We need new programs to help the poor and opportunities to challenge the young. There has to be a plan for growth — only then will fairness result. My husband's experience exemplifies growth and the successful passage of opportunity to the next generation. His success indicates inclusion rather than division. My husband offers a new direction, welcoming change, prosperity and greater cooperation among peoples and nations. Donald intends to represent all the people, not just some of the people. That includes Christians and Jews and

Muslims, it includes Hispanics and African-Americans and Asians, and the poor and the middle class. Throughout his career, Donald has successfully worked with people of many faiths and with many nations.

Like no one else, I have seen the talent, the energy, the tenacity, the resourceful mind and the simple goodness of heart that God gave Donald Trump. Now is the time to use those gifts as never before, for purposes far greater than ever before. And he will do this better than anyone else can... and it won't even be close. Everything depends on it, for our cause and for our country. People are counting on him — all the millions of you who have touched us so much with your kindness and your confidence. You have turned this unlikely campaign into a movement that is still gaining in strength and number. The primary season, and its toughness, is behind us.

Let's all come together in a national campaign like no other! The race will be hard-fought, all the way to November. There will be good times and hard times and unexpected turns — it would not be a Trump contest without excitement and drama. But through it all, my husband will remain focused on only one thing: this beautiful country that he loves so much. If I am honored to serve as first lady, I will use that wonderful privilege to try to help people in our country who need it the most. One of the many causes dear to my heart is helping children and women. You judge a society by how it treats its citizens. We must do our best to ensure that every child can live in comfort and security, with the best possible education. As citizens of this great nation, it is kindness, love and compassion for each other that will bring us together — and keep us together. These are the values Donald and I will bring to the White House. My husband is ready to lead this great nation. He is ready to fight, every day, to give our children the better future they deserve. Ladies and gentlemen, Donald J. Trump is ready to serve and lead this country as the next president of the United States. Thank you, God bless you, and God bless America.

8. Conclusion

It's easy to see the dramatic change in her personality and confidence by comparing the two speeches from this book. Thanks to her most recent speech, more people are getting interested in the Presidential campaign and picking and rooting for their sides with vigor. All of the recent controversies and parodies surrounding her are actually playing a huge role in increasing her popularity. We still have a few months to see whether the Trumps will make it to the White House or not, but we will all agree unanimously that it will be one of the most exciting and entertaining campaigns that we've ever experienced.

I'd like to sign off with a quote from Melania's speech. "There will be good times and hard times and unexpected turns — it would not be a Trump contest without excitement and drama."

The End

About the author

Born and raised in New York, Talia Rose has always been an avid reader since childhood. Hence, becoming a writer was the natural path for her to take. She has an open mind and is always ready to learn from the inspiring stories of others. Besides her daily trips to Starbucks and the strolls down Central Park, her most favorite activity is to entertain her readers through her writings.

Made in the USA
Lexington, KY
07 February 2017